ISBN 978-0-656-76963-6
PIBN 10482471

OBSERVATIONS

ON THE

PAPERS

LATELY

SUBMITTED TO PARLIAMENT

UPON THE SUBJECT

OF THE

Affairs of Portugal.

LONDON:

EDWARD BULL, HOLLES STREET.

1830.

OBSERVATIONS,

&c.

THE consideration of the papers submitted to Parliament, respecting the relations between Great Britain and Portugal, having been interrupted by the close of the last Session, it has been thought that an analysis of their contents, combined with a short recapitulation of the events which they record, might not be misplaced at the present moment. Attention cannot but revive to a subject not less intimately connected with the interests of the British Nation, than with the character of its Government; and if this publication should aid the enquiries of those who are disposed to investigate it, the object with which it is written will be fully answered. It is to be borne in mind, that the documents laid before Parliament, are less to be considered as an impartial statement of events, than as the garbled defence of a Ministry, whose exclusive access to the originals, enables them, by quoting some passages and suppressing others, to mould the meaning to their own purposes.

Extracts without reference to context or sequel, are always weak and often perverted evidence. Even out of these however, by careful examination, and by comparison with known facts, some truth may be picked to the elucidation of transactions, which have been easily tolerated, only because they have been little understood.

The extract laid before Parliament, from the first of Sir Charles Stewart's dispatches, gives us to understand, though it does not distinctly state, that he recommended to Don Pedro, to grant to Portugal a constitutional system, founded on the ancient institutions of the country, rather than one emanating from his own imagination.

By the extract from his second dispatch, it appears that Sir Charles offered advice to Don Pedro, as to the time of publishing the decree by which the Charter was accorded, and as to the period of its communication at Lisbon.

The third extract, and the remainder of the second, relate to the mode of conveying the Charter to Lisbon; whereby it appears, that Sir Charles, after making some difficulties on the 30th of April, consented on the 1st of May, to be the bearer of it himself. Here is enough to shew, that the Charter was framed in some sort with the concurrence of the British Ambassador, and that Don Pedro conformed to his notions upon the subject, in as far as was necessary for the purpose of inducing him to be the bearer of it to Portugal.

It was impossible after this act, for Sir Charles to disconnect himself from it, nor could the Government he represented, divest itself of equal participation in the measure, unless by a prompt and public disavowal of the proceedings of its Ambassador. So far from a disavowal, Sir Charles's conduct in bringing the Charter, met with entire approbation, and he was directed to come home, in order " that we might inculcate more strongly " on other governments the duty of abstaining from " any interference with the free agency of Portu- " gal ;"* that is to say, in order to prevent the interposition of any external impediment in the way of the adoption of the constitution which had been granted to her.

This approbation is an explicit answer to the silly notion which has been attempted to be propagated, of Sir Charles having acted, in making himself the bearer of the Charter, as a Portuguese plenipotentiary, and not as a British ambassador. If this separation of characters had been possible, if it had been recognised at the time, no approbation from the British Government would have been wanted for an act performed by him as a functionary of another state. This after-invention, however, was not then devised ; it was felt that Sir Charles had incurred a heavy responsibility, (whereof he appears by the extract from his second dispatch,

* Mr. Canning, of July 12.

to have been himself aware at the time,) and the British Government adopting his views, and sanctioning his conveyance of the Charter, sent him, without loss of time, a full approval of his conduct.* In the dispatch containing this approval, the arguments which shou'd decide the Portuguese government and nation to the acceptance of the Charter, are elaborately set forth. These are " The necessity for a convocation of the " Cortes in some shape or other." The preference to be accorded to a constitutional Charter rather than to the convocation of an ancient assembly. The hope that the continental courts " will ab- " stain from opposition to a measure, the rejec- " tion whereof, in Portugal, would revive all the " difficulties that have been just overcome, and " would place the crown of Portugal, and not the " crown only, but the monarchy itself of Brazil in " danger."

These are strong words of advice from a British Government to a Portuguese Regency, leaning at that time exclusively upon England for support, and acting in all things by her recommendation. Nor was this dispatch likely to be barren, addressed as it was to the bearer of the constitution—to the man the most interested in its adoption, whose diplomatic reputation was in a manner bound up with its success. At least this reasoning, the ex-

* Mr. Canning, No. 5, July 12.

pression of the sentiments of the British Cabinet, conveyed through its official organ, was not addressed to a Portuguese plenipotentiary.

It is the correspondence of His Majesty's Secretary of State with a British Ambassador, and by that Ambassador, in the course of his duty, it must have been communicated to the Government then existing in Portugal; nor was this likely to be done in a manner to derogate from its weight. With such a document upon record, to contend that the British Government was no party to the establishment of the Constitution in Portugal, is a degree of absurdity only to be equalled by its baseness and want of faith.

The cause assigned in a dispatch of the same date to Sir W. A'Court, for calling Sir Charles Stuart home, is more explicit than that alleged to Sir Charles himself; it is therein stated to be, the expediency of contradicting " a foolish notion which " had got abroad in France, that Sir Charles's " powers from the Emperor of Brazil, amounted to " the constituting His Excellency a member of the Regency of Portugal."* This then precisely defines the grounds of jealousy as to the exertion of British influence on so momentous an occasion, which it is stated to be " particularly expedient to " remove;"† and thus it appears from Mr. Canning's correspondence, that the recall of Sir Charles Stuart

---

* Mr. Canning, No. 6, 12 July.

† Mr. Canning, No. 5, 12 July.

neither arose from any lurking disapprobation of his conduct, nor from a wish in the British Government to disconnect itself from the Portuguese Charter, of the adoption of which, on the contrary, it made itself, as early as the 12th of July, the unhesitating advocate and adviser. This indeed was done so explicitly, and to such an extent, that the instruction to Sir Charles Stuart, whereof the tendency has been already examined, was at the same time communicated to Sir W. A'Court, our Ambassador at the court of Lisbon, " as addressed equally to him- " self, and as the guide of his language in commu- " nicating with the government to which he was " accredited, and with his diplomatic colleagues."

Now as it is impossible that Mr. Canning could have directed a language to be held by his Majesty's Ambassador in Portugal, to his diplomatic colleagues, which should be at variance with that spoken at the same time by himself to the agents of the same Courts accredited in England, it follows, that at that period, he had made himself the advocate of the adoption of the Charter, with all the European courts, with which communication was had upon the subject. How in the face of these documents the Ministers can have subsequently contended that the British Government was no party to the establishment of the constitutional Charter in Portugal, is beyond comprehension. Parties by their Ambassador to its construction, and conveyance to Europe, and directly by themselves to its adoption in Portugal, how could they have been more parties to it?

Their assertion to the contrary would almost induce a belief, that they had not taken the trouble to make themselves acquainted with the contents of the papers they have produced, were it not that many of them, (and among them the Duke of Wellington) were members of the cabinet, by which the transactions of that period were directed, and that thus his Grace's influence must then have been as active and as decisive to the establishment of the constitution, as it has since been to its overthrow.

Clear and distinct as are the recommendations already recited, they yet did not suffice for the anxiety which the British cabinet at that time felt for the adoption of the Charter in Portugal.

On the 17th Mr. Canning again wrote to Sir W. A'Court, inclosing to him, for communication to the Portuguese minister for foreign affairs, copies of dispatches, to his Majesty's agents at foreign courts, shewing " with what anxious perseverance " his Majesty's government was labouring to create " in other powers a disposition favourable to the " peace and security of Portugal;" that is to say, according to the explanations afforded by his previous dispatches, " inculcating upon them the duty " of abstaining from any interference with the free " agency of Portugal;" while he at the same time, lest any doubt should exist as to the direction in which England wished that free agency to be ex-

erted, offers (with only as much of a disclaimer of a settled opinion or of peremptory advice, as might render counsel not unpalatable to an independent state,) " the distinct opinion of his Majesty's Go-
" vernment* that the best chance of a safe and tran-
" quil issue to the crisis, will be found in the ac-
" ceptance as immediate, as may be suitable with
" the importance of the measure, of the Charter of
" Don Pedro, coupled as it is with his abdication
" of the crown ;" and he adds, that " any other
" course must, as it appears to us, be full of
" danger." Could any thing short of " peremptory
" advice," (by which something little less than an order is to be understood,) be more distinct or decisive. Yet that no link may be wanting ; to this strong series of recommendations is superadded the accounts of the effect thereby produced in Sir W. A'Court's reply of July 29. In this he states the receipt of Mr. Canning's dispatch of the 17th, its communication to the Infanta, enhanced by his own comments upon " the great interest displayed in ·
" favour of Portugal by his Majesty's Government,
" and by Mr. Canning's endeavours to give a right
" direction to the policy of Europe on the present
" occasion ;" and announces as the result, that the execution of the Emperor's orders, which had been retarded, is gradually proceeding, and that " the
" swearing to the constitution, would begin on the
" Monday following."

* Mr. Canning, No. 7, 17th July.

Here then is the distinct avowal that to a dispatch from the British Secretary of State, and to the use made of it by a British Ambassador, was due the solution of a question which had before been undecided, and the consequent fixing of a day for the fulfilment of the recommendation it had conveyed, is announced with the triumphant brevity of a man who has carried a point prescribed to him by his Government.

Between these two dispatches there intervenes one from Sir Charles Stuart of the 15th of July, giving an account of the hesitations of the Regent, and of the encouragement which he had given to her Royal Highness to proceed in the execution of Don Pedro's orders, to which he adds his own anticipations of success. This document might be important, if the decisive communications before cited, did not take away all interest from this subordinate piece. It serves however, to show, that from the moment of Sir Charles Stuart's landing at Lisbon, there was no period at which the English influence was inactive, in counselling in some shape or other the adoption of the Charter he had brought. In this interval there had taken place a correspondence of greater importance, addressed by Mr. Canning to Sir W. A'Court and Sir Charles Stuart; one indeed which, by evincing an uncalled-for anxiety in the British cabinet to shield itself from reproach, appears to mark a commencement of indecision, which, in the hands of the present Ministers, has

degenerated into a system of shifting and tergiver-
sation, as little creditable to the nation that has
permitted it, as to the individuals who have carried
it on. Whether moved by appearances on the
continent, or shrinking from responsibility at home,
the British Government, without waiting for an
answer to its dispatch of the 17th, sent an extra
packet on the 22d, for the purpose of expressing to
Sir W. A'Court, " An anxious wish that nothing
" may have been done at Lisbon which can be liable
" to be misconstrued as an authoritative interference
" in the internal concerns of Portugal ; and should
" any thing of the sort have occurred, Sir W.
" A'Court is directed, by a discreet use of the ex-
" planations and declarations contained in Mr.
" Canning's former dispatches, to explain it away."
Now the real meaning and result of his former dis-.
patches, has been already set forth, and the discreet use of them here prescribed, can only intend a
perversion of their simple meaning, and a new
colour to be adroitly given to the acts, which, in
obedience to them Sir W. A'Court might have already performed.

The term " authoritative interference" is evi-
dently intended to afford a loophole for escape
from the responsibility attached to the part we
had been playing, but the distinction cannot be
sustained ; the Regency, which had directed the
affairs of Portugal, after the death of John the
Sixth, had been named by that king only a few

days before his demise ; during several days before the signature of the instrument by which it
was constituted, his Majesty had been incapable of
doing any act whatever ; those who asserted its
validity contended that it had been executed during
an interval of amelioration, but the opposite party
were loud in their contradiction of the fact, and in
their assertions of its nullity. The Regency was
by it confided to a Council presided by one of his
younger daughters, to the exclusion of the Queen,
his widow ; of the Infant, Don Miguel ; and of his
eldest daughter, a widow, residing in Spain. To
a party headed by such claimants, and backed by
the power of Spain, what had a Regency acting
under a disputed title to oppose after the arrival of
the Charter ?—an army discontented, and desert-
ing by whole regiments into Spain ; a clergy
leagued with its opponents, and directing the
opinions of the mass of the people ; a body of ma-
gistrates and judges trembling for the duration of
their own salaries and power, the constant enemies
of all innovation or improvement. In Portugal,
and on the continent, the Regency had no element
of support whereon to rely; its sole chance of conti-
nuance depended on the countenance and protection
of England. In such a state of things, the recommendation, though not authoritatively given, could
not fail to be attended to ; nor is it too much to
assert, that unless the Charter had been brought
from Brazil, no attempt at framing one would

at that time have arisen in Portugal ; that if it had come by other hands it would have been at once rejected ; and that, unless recommended by the British Government, it would not have been finally adopted or put in operation.

The dispatch of the same date* to Sir Charles Stuart is merely a more pressing repetition of the order to return home, for the reasons which had been before assigned. It needs no examination, and is without weight on the judgment to be formed in the affair.

One contingency alone existed, under which the tardy and half-avowed attempt at retractation, conveyed in Mr. Canning's dispatch of July 22nd, could have been effective to its purpose. It was that of the previous dispatch of the 17th not having been received in time to be acted upon before the arrival of the succeeding one. This contingency failed. Mr. Canning's dispatch of the 22nd, forwarded by the extra packet, reached Sir W. A'Court one hour after the Lyra had sailed with his reply to that of the 17th.† The announcement of the victory he had obtained, crossed in the mouth of the Tagus, with the modification of the orders under which the battle had been fought. And how does he reply to the new directions to which he was then directed to conform? " He " cannot deny that there has been interference, a

* July 22.   † Sir W. A'Court, No. 1, August 4.

" very direct and active interference in the affairs " of Portugal;" but he draws a distinction as to the persons by whom it has been exerted, assuring his Principal, that " whatever may be said of the " Portuguese Plenipotentiary, the British Ambas- " sador is responsible for nothing." Could it, however, have escaped Sir W. A'Court that Sir Charles Stuart was also a British Ambassador, and that the disjunction of two characters in one and the same person is not always clear or intel- ligible?—that although " his colleagues and the " Portuguese Government might not be mistaken " as to the difference in the parts which the two " British Ambassadors were called upon to play," they were yet liable, and authorized to put their own interpretation upon the motives for which these two parts were enacted, and that the mass of the Portuguese nation, and the enlightened portion of the inhabitants of Europe, who had not been admitted behind the scenes, might be but too well entitled, when the catastrophe should come, to look upon the whole management as a juggle,

> " To keep the word of promise to the ear,
> " But break it to the hope."

What, however, shall be said if it should prove, upon investigation, that this device of a Portuguese Plenipotentiary was altogether a fiction, having no real foundation?

Sir Charles Stuart had indeed been invested with that character to the Emperor of Brazil, but by what process had he, upon his return to Lisbon, undergone a change into a Portuguese Plenipotentiary to Portugal itself? It has hitherto been understood, that an Ambassador having completed a special commission, and being returned to the Court from which it had been received, was thereby divested of the character with which he had been cloathed, re-entering at once the walk of private life. At most, if it had so pleased the Regent of Portugal, it lay with her Royal Highness to continue to Sir Charles Stuart the character which he had borne, of her Plenipotentiary to the Emperor of Brazil; but this was not done, and if it had been, what faculty, what qualification could it have given to him to advise her upon the interests of her own kingdom?

As Portuguese plenipotentiary he could have neither eyes to see, nor tongue to speak; but as the court from which his commission was received, should instruct him. The character of Ambassador from the Emperor of Brazil had not been conferred upon him. During his residence at Lisbon, he retained no public situation but that which he had not yet deposed, of Ambassador from England, nor without the weight which he derived from it. Would he have been listened to for a moment? Here, then, this shallow subterfuge may be dismissed; its adoption only marks the shifts to which those who could have recourse to it were driven, in preparing for evasion or defence. Even with the advantage of this fictitious distinction of parts, Sir W. A'Court can bring himself to say no more, than that " He thinks he can safely assert, " that the British Government has never been com- " mitted either by Sir Charles Stuart, or by him- " self."

Not committed to what? to an authoritative in- terference he must mean ; for the order to interfere by recommendation, by strong and closely rea- soned recommendation, had not been withdrawn, and to deny that to this extent the orders of his Government had been acted upon, would be to fly in the face of his own dispatch, then only six days' old, giving an account of his audience with the Regent, of his communication at that audience of the opinions and efforts of his Government, and of the victorious result in the consequent appoint- ment of a day for swearing to the constitution. The British Government was committed by the orders it had sent—by the use that had been made of them—by the public acts which had ensued ; nor could any subsequent retractation annul the con- nexion with the Charter, which of its own free will it had sought and cemented. The union was in- dissoluble, there remained only that it should be borne with credit.

Here ends the first act of this tragedy, and here ended also for the time, the attempt of the British government to recede from the position it had taken. Circumstances at this period combined in such a manner as to induce it to step forward by acts in defence of that free agency of Portugal which it had begun by inculcating in words. Upon these circumstances the papers before us are silent; but in order to continue the chain of events, it may be well shortly to state, that in the first days of December, 1826, a general attack was made upon Portugal, by the Portuguese refugees, who had fled into Spain. And that by the 1st of January, 1827, a British force sent to the assistance of the Regent, had anchored in the Tagus. The instructions given to the officer commanding that force, are not produced; but they cannot have been inconsistent with the language held by Mr. Canning in Parliament. In his speech, published by himself, and therefore to be regarded as the deliberate opinion of the British cabinet, expressed through its official organ in the affairs immediately entrusted to his charge, in this speech, uncontradicted and unmodified by any one of his colleagues.* " As an English

* Mr. Canning, in his Speech on the 1st of May, 1829, after expressing his astonishment that his late colleagues should suddenly decline acting with him, applies the following expressions to the secession of Mr. Peel : " Between my Right Ho-
" nourable friend and myself, it is almost unnecessary for me
" to observe, that upon every subject in every discussion I can
" call to mind upon all great questions of foreign or domestic
" policy and legislation (the Catholic question alone excepted,)
" there has been that sort of general agreement, that I do not

" Minister," he says, " may God prosper this at-
" tempt at the establishment of constitutional liberty
" in Portugal ; and may that nation be found as fit
" to enjoy and to cherish its new-born privileges, as
" it has often proved itself capable of discharging
" its duties amongst the nations of the world.   To
" that constitution, unquestioned in its origin, for
" it is admitted on all hands to have proceeded
" from a legitimate source, even by those who are
" most jealous of new institutions—to that consti-
" tution founded on principles similar to those of
" our own, though differently modified, it is im-
" possible that Englishmen should not wish well."

Such was the encouragement, which, in dis-
claiming the intention of " imposing the Charter
" by a forcible interference," the British Government yet expressed towards the constitution and its
partisans.   The nation re-echoed the appeal.   It
was backed by the immediate departure of the expedition for Lisbon, and England upraised herself

" Like a great sea mark, standing every flaw,
" And saving those that eyed her."

The struggle between the troops of the Regent
and the rebels, lasted upon different points, and
with various success, for nearly three months.   The
presence of the British army at Lisbon during this
period, by securing the capital, enabled the Regent

" believe there exists the individual with whom my opinions
" are in more complete accordance."

to employ the whole of her disposable force in active operations in the field; but even this assistance, considerable as it was, was not found sufficiently decisive to insure success to her arms, or to arouse an uncompromising co-operation from a people, made wary by experience, and acquainted with the sufferings, which result from changes in the possession and employment of power.

In the middle of January a part of the British force advanced towards the Mondego, and in February, when after the failure of the attack upon Oporto, the whole of the rebel forces were concentrated in the north; and when the road from Chaves was open to them for an attack, either on Oporto or Lisbon, a British division took post at Coimbra, and by its presence there, contributed to determine the retreat of the rebels into Spain, where, on the 22d of February, they were disarmed.

Thus did the movement of a British corps assist in deciding the issue of a contest, which had been doubtful as long as it had remained inactive; and thus was the constitution, which had been proclaimed in conformity to our counsels, indirectly established by our arms. The Portuguese, who had hitherto doubted of the extent to which our co-operation might be depended upon, were determined by this apparently overt act of assistance, and the constitutional party, which, up to this period had been faint, backward, and hesitating, threw doubt and indecision away, and from that hour assumed an uncontested ascendancy in the direction of affairs. It was checked in its exercise only by the interference of the British Ambassador, constantly exerted to moderate all proceedings which appeared likely to give umbrage to the continental powers. To an intimation of the wishes of England, every other consideration uniformly give way. If her support in the hour of danger had been the reward of this deference, it would have been worth the price that was paid for it, but when the Portuguese Constitutionalists were subsequently abandoned, it became doubtful whether the free course which their enthusiasm would have taken, had they been left to themselves, would not better have prepared them for defence, against the attacks of their enemies. The period thus irreparably thrown away, comprised nearly a year, during which the influence of England was all powerful, and during which, nothing was done to give solidity to the system which had been adopted. On the 3d of July, 1827, Don Pedro signed a decree, naming the Infant Don Miguel, his lieutenant in Portugal, and at the same time his Imperial Majesty wrote, both to the King of England and to the Emperor of Austria, requesting those sovereigns to provide that the constitutional Charter might continue to be the fundamental law of that kingdom.*

In October began the conferences at Vienna,

* Vide Enclosures in No. 15.

which prepared the way for the return of Don Miguel to Portugal.

The first question to be asked, with respect to these conferences, relates to the right by which they were held at all. With respect to the expediency there was no doubt. It was expedient that the credit of England should be saved—that the party she had compromised in Portugal should not be exposed— that the fabric she had raised should not be violently overthrown—that her ancient connexion with Portugal should not be dissolved, nor all power in that country transferred at once from the hands of her devoted adherents into those of a sworn enemy. The expediency was clear, but where was the right? and where was the principle of non-interference when these protocols were framed?—when the conditions upon which Don Miguel should be allowed to return to the country he had been appointed to govern, were placed in discussion?—when it was announced to him, by the minister of Austria, acting in concert with England, that unless he consented to return by the route appointed for him, he should not be allowed to return, till a fresh reference had been made to the Emperor, his brother— which was well understood by Don Miguel, as being equivalent to his never being allowed to return at all—where was our principle of not interfering while these things were doing ?* Did it sleep, or was it forgotten ? Upon this point, it lies with the Go-

* Letter of Prince Metternich, Oct. 18.

vernment to reconcile its practice with its profes-
sions ; let it however be understood, that this in-
consistency is only exposed in order to shew the
falseness of the pretences, under which the Government has veiled its connivance in other instances,
not to reproach it with the interference exerted in
this. That interference was just, was necessary,
and gave a promise of good, never destined to be
realized.

In the protocols drawn up at Vienna, Don Miguel pledged himself by his plenipotentiaries " to
" maintain religiously the institutions of Portu-
" gal, and to bury what had passed in oblivion."
Amnesty and the Charter were the conditions required for his return, and to those he solemnly
bound himself. In return, Austria and England
engaged to obtain from Don Pedro " the confirma-
" tion of his act of abdication, the sending of the
" Queen Maria da Gloria to Portugal, and the total
" and definitive separation of the two crowns."*
The engagements taken by Austria and England
were fulfilled, but when Don Miguel failed in those
to which he had bound himself in return, the British Government pretended to discover that the
enforcing them, would be an interference in the
affairs of a foreign and independent state. Why
in God's name, at what period of these transactions, had they not interfered ? and why was their
interference to cease, at the precise moment when

* Protocol of Oct. 20th.

it had been legalized by the signature of a protocol equivalent to a treaty, and when its cessation was to deliver the friends and adherents of England, those who had acted at her instigation, the agents of her will, and now the victims of her caprice, to the dungeon, and the torture, and the scaffold? It is a hateful recollection, and a stain upon her fair fame, which neither time nor repentance can efface.

Besides the engagements taken in the protocols, Don Miguel further bound himself by a letter, addressed directly from himself to the King of England, to the maintenance of the institutions given by Don Pedro, and to the cultivation of the ancient alliance between Great Britain and Portugal. Thus did His Majesty find himself invested with a sort of guardianship of these institutions, first by the delegation given to him to that effect by Don Pedro in his letter of July 3d; and secondly, by the engagement voluntarily taken towards him by Don Miguel in that of October 19th: nor were these demonstrations on the part of the Infant devoid of effect. They served to procure for him a reception in England, which paved the way for a similar one in Portugal; they served to lull the constitutional party, and to dissuade it from concerting measures either for eventual resistance or for timely security.

Upon what passed during the residence of Don Miguel in England the documents are silent. It has, however, been understood that upon his re-

.newing his engagements it was determined to furnish him with money, and to prolong the stay of the army in Portugal. He sailed early in February, and before the end of that month he arrived in Lisbon.

From this time till the departure of Sir Frederick Lamb from Lisbon in July, the daily encroachments and final usurpation of Don Miguel are detailed in the published correspondence of that Ambassador; but we look in vain therein for an account of the persecutions exercised either towards the native Portuguese or towards British subjects; and as little do we perceive a trace in them of any efforts made by the British government, or by its Ambassador, to obtain for them protection or redress, or to fulfil the still more imperious duty of summoning Don Miguel to respect his public engagements, and to give security and confidence to individuals by an undeviating adherence to the amnesty, to which his faith had been solemnly pledged. Sir Frederick Lamb appears to have contented himself with the ineffective salvo of the majority of the nation being desirous that Don Miguel should declare himself king;* an assumption which turned out to be false, and was retracted by himself in a dispatch written only eight days later, wherein he states that, " in spite of all the efforts that have been " used, no success has been obtained towards in-

* Sir F. Lamb, No. 18, March 14.

" ducing the country to declare itself for proclaim-
" ing him king."* If the first assertion had been
correct, in what way would it have affected the
question? When was it ever held that the worth
and weight of a nation were represented by a mere
numerical majority? and by what new and dange-
rous doctrine can the right of conferring crowns
and sanctioning usurpation be attributed to it?
Yet even were this admitted, what influence could
it have had upon Don Miguel's engagements to
England? It was over them that the Ambassador
was more particularly bound to watch; and an intimation from us that we were determined to enforce the observance of the protocols, to which we
were parties, would have stopped persecution in the
outset, and usurpation could never have been heard
of. Was it given? Has the Government got it
to produce? And, if not, why has it not? These
are questions that must be answered. Upon the
sending back the money, upon the stopping the
departure of the army from Lisbon, something
must have passed. Why was the sailing of the
British force countermanded; and, having been so,
why was that counter-order revoked? It is evident that the case is as yet but half explained;
and till it shall be fully so, the conduct of the Government in this part of the transaction cannot be
fairly judged: but this may be said already, that

* Sir F. Lamb, No. 23, March 22.

by the sincerity of its efforts to cause the engagements to which it was a party to be respected, and
not only by their sincerity, but by the foresight
with which they were conceived, by the firmness
and perseverance with which they were exerted,
must the Government be condemned or absolved.
If their measures were wanting in any of these
requisites, they failed in capacity to watch over the
interests of a great nation; if wilfully wanting in
them they betrayed them.

One circumstance, of which no mention is made
in Sir F. Lamb's dispatches, would augur ill for
the real intentions of the Government. It is, the
admitted fact, that from the period of Don Miguel's
landing in Portugal, a correspondence was carried
on, with the privity of the Duke of Wellington,
between Lord Beresford and certain persons deep
in the confidence of the Queen Mother and of the
Infant, and immediately attached to their persons.

It was well known at Lisbon, that the Portuguese
ministers gave implicit confidence to the contents
of this correspondence, paying little attention to
what came through official channels. It is well
known, that several Portuguese officers who attached themselves to the cause of Don Miguel,
have since declared, that they did so in consequence
of letters which were shewn to them from Lord Beresford; and so little did his correspondents conceal,
at the time, the purport of their communications
with him, that they made it publicly current in

Lisbon, that he was in the habit of going with their letters to the Duke of Wellington, early on the morning of their arrival, so that his Grace received his first notions through this foul channel, and was in the habit of communicating information, upon Portuguese affairs, to his Secretary for the foreign department, instead of receiving it from him. It is true, that the proceedings of Lord Beresford were so notorious as to attract the notice of Parliament, which drew a faint and equivocal disclaimer from the Duke of Wellington, intimating that his Lordship was unauthorized by him. His explanation was unsatisfactory, nor could any one understand how a Premier, who visited the slightest insubordination with instantaneous dismissal, should overlook such an act of indiscipline in the most subservient of his creatures. These things have a bad appearance; it is for the Government to clear itself from the suspicion which they have thrown upon it, by the production of evidence to their conduct. The honour of the nation is too deeply implicated in the transaction, for us not to hope that this evidence may be found to be more satisfactory than we should at present be warranted in anticipating.

The rest of the published documents relate to the demand made by the Marquis of Barbacena, for assistance to the young Queen of Portugal, and to the affairs of Terceira. In the Marquis of Barbacena's letter, several points are enforced, strongly confirmatory of the view which has just been taken of the case ; while in the whole correspondence, on the part of the British Ministers, there is but one argument urged, which, if admitted, would in the least tend to invalidate it.

This argument is to be found in the Earl of Aberdeen's reply of January 13th, 1829, wherein his Lordship asserts, that " the assurance given to " Don Miguel, and entered upon the protocol of " the conference, to offer to the Emperor Don " Pedro, certain advice, does not render His Ma- " jesty the guarantee of the performance of those " promises contained in the letters of Don Miguel, " which were laid before the conference, and an- " nexed to the protocol. Neither does the advice " tendered to the Emperor, upon the propriety of " the execution of these important acts, respecting " which his Imperial Majesty had long before " pledged his royal word, confer any right what- " ever of claiming from His Majesty those succours " which are necessary for the conquest of Portu- " gal." This is rather the reasoning of an attorney than of a statesman, yet, even technically considered, it is incorrect.

The facts are simply these. The British Government was called in to arbitrate the conditions of Don Miguel's return to Portugal.

In return for certain stipulations entered into by His Royal Highness, it undertook to obtain for him concessions of high importance from Don Pedro.

It fulfilled its engagement: but Don Miguel failed in his part of the compact.

The arbitrating power was then called upon by Don Pedro, to assist in compelling the fulfilment of the bargain.

The appeal was vain, for the arbitrating power shifted from itself the obligation to enforce the execution of the very engagements, by pleading which, it had obtained from Don Pedro the required concessions. The plea upon which this was done, was that of not having formally guaranteed their performance; and also because " Don Pedro had " before pledged his royal word to grant them," as though they had been less obtained by our intervention, because his Imperial Majesty had seen cause to defer their fulfilment until he should have a sufficient guarantee for the future conduct of his brother; which guarantee he supposed to be com · plete when the British Government had made itself a party to the transactions between them.

If in private life the obtaining any thing under false pretences is rightly denominated swindling, it will be difficult to shew, by what other term the conduct of the British Government, as described by Lord Aberdeen in this transaction is to be designated. An attempt has been made in another place to pervert this plain view of the question by the assertion that the British Ambassador had signed the protocols of Vienna only as a witness.

There is no example of a signature so given or

so understood, unless it were so specified in the instrument. Moreover in these protocols the Ambassador undertook certain obligations on the part of England. This was the act of a principal. The doing it would have disqualified him for a witness —how then could he have been a witness, only? The assertion is unworthy of further examination. Yet a much more elaborate refutation of it, may be seen in the Marquis of Barbacena's letter of the 25th of November. We cannot quit the subject of that nobleman's correspondence, without reverting to the inaccurate taunt already quoted from Lord Aberdeen's reply to him, " that no right has been con-
" ferred of claiming from his Majesty those succours
" which are necessary for the conquest of Portugal."
As though such had been the demand of the Marquis of Barbacena, or that conquest, and succours to an ally for a specific object, were synonymous terms. This taunt, however, may perhaps be regarded less as an attempt to alter the nature of the question, than as an ebullition of temper, not unnatural, when we reflect, that if good faith had never been more entirely sacrificed to the passions and prejudices of individuals, neither had it ever been more unrequitedly so: their own minion having turned round upon them with every aggravation of insult and contempt, and their country, whose interests they had abandoned along with its honour, having reaped but the shame of political dishonesty, without its advantages.

In the discussion between the Marquis of Barbacena and the Earl of Aberdeen, it is natural that, no claimant upon the assistance of the British Government should be brought forwards, except Don Pedro, acting on behalf of his daughter. But could the British Secretary of State, in considering this question, have overlooked the claims of another party—those of the Portuguese Constitutionalists? Could he have failed to recall to mind, that the signature of a British Ambassador to the protocols, had given to their stipulations a weight in Portugal, which without it they would have wanted? Could he be unmindful that, after their completion, assurances of safety had been transmitted from Vienna, through the British Ambassador at Lisbon, to some of the leaders of the constitutional party, for the purpose, and with the effect of inducing them to lay aside the resolution they had taken to quit Portugal? Did it not occur to him, that the reception given to Don Miguel, in England; that the leaving the British force at Lisbon, for more than a year, after all apprehension of invasion from Spain had ceased; that the withdrawing it at the moment when the designs of the Infant were unmasked, had had the effect, (whatever might have been the intention) of delivering the party with which we had been acting, unprepared, betrayed, and blindfolded into his hands? Could his Lordship dissemble these things to himself, or, seeing the lamentable state to which thousands had been thereby reduced, could he look upon their sufferings without pity, and without a wish to exercise the right and the power he possessed to interfere efficaciously in their behalf, because, forsooth, they were constitutionalists, and therefore, according to some notion of his own, no friends to England?—strange as the answer may sound, it is to be feared that it must be in the affirmative. The more closely this painful subject is examined into, the worse does it appear. Let us return to the consideration of the published documents. The remainder of these refer, as has been stated, to the demand for assistance to the young Queen, and to the affair of Terceira; episodes in the great drama which has been acting, but episodes, wherein the undisguised hostility of the English Government to the constitutional party, breaks avowedly forth; which contrast strangely with its opening scenes, when the Charter was to be recommended and maintained, and wherein it is difficult to decide, whether public right in action, or private courtesy in expression, were most disregarded. If however it be true, as we think it has been proved, that the Portuguese constitution did not originate in Portugal ; that it would neither have been adopted there, unless recommended—nor sustained, unless supported—by us; that we had stipulated for its integrity before we permitted Don Miguel to take possession of the Regency ; that upon the faith of his promise, the veto was withdrawn which had before been placed upon his departure from Austria; that in consequence of his engagements, we solicited and

obtained concessions in his favour from Don Pedro, ·
which had, up to that time, been withheld from him;
that by our assurances and shew of confidence in
him, we lulled the apprehensions of the party,
which at that time possessed all power in Portugal,
and dissuaded it from measures of self-defence or
flight ; surely a very different defence is required to
clear us, from any which has hitherto been made; nor
until that defence be seen, can we wonder at the im-
pression produced in Europe by the presence throughout it of thousands of Portuguese, many of them
of the highest station and endowments, driven from
their homes, reduced to poverty, and rendered
outcasts upon the face of the earth, from no as-
signable cause but their condescendence to British advice, and their reliance upon British consistency. Such a result demands either a satisfactory explanation or a sufficient atonement. It
is for the Parliament to exact one or the other :
let us hope that its duty will be fulfilled.

It must be evident to all who reason upon the
subject, that the Portuguese Charter has been
throughout, the symbol, and not the object of the
contest to which it has given rise. Through Portugal
Spain was aimed at ; nor is it improbable, that in
the final result, an union of the whole of the west of
Europe, under representative constitutions more or
less analogous to that of England, was remotely
contemplated. Such an object, although often
disclaimed by the ministry of 1826, whereof Lord

Liverpool was the head, was yet perfectly consistent with the spirit in which that government was administered. Their policy was directed to two great points: to liberate Spain from French troops and French influence, and to obtain her recognition of South American independence.

To these results, no way led so directly as the introduction of a constitutional system into Spain; nor could a mode be found so likely to induce its adoption there, as the example of its success in Portugal. The British Ministry could not have been so blind to the necessary effects of the moral and geographical relations of those countries as to suppose that they could long continue to be governed under such conflicting systems without clashing. They could not fail to arrive, within no distant interval, either by consent or by force, either to avoid collision, or, in consequence of it, at a system which should place the institutions of the two kingdoms in harmony with each other.

England, which erected the constitutional standard in Portugal, must have been prepared to insure to it the victory. It was a vast and perilous enterprise, but not without its chances of success—a success which the subsequent course of events in France would have insured to it. The battle, however, was suspended before it had well begun. The British Ministry of 1828, instead of combating under the standard of their predecessors, erected an opposite one—that of a return, in as far as should be possible, to the state of things which had existed before the French Revolution. Should it be asked upon what grounds this assertion is made—let the ministry of Monsieur de Polignac in France—let the resistance to the emancipation of Greece—let the connivance at the Spanish expedition for the subjugation of Mexico—let the protection accorded to an usurper in Portugal, answer.

It is foreign to the present purpose to examine which of these opposite systems is to be preferred; but if the interests of England and of humanity could leave the decision doubtful, yet might the question be solved by the consideration in either case of the possibility of success. It is the characteristic of a statesman to attempt nothing which cannot be attained, and so to connect and combine the measures to which his peculiar views may incline him, with the progress of opinion and the spirit of the times he lives in, as in a manner to amalgamate them together, and produce in the result a whole, which shall work without shocks or sudden changes, and by satisfying in some measure all interests, unite them all in its support.

The system which has been acted upon by the British Government since 1828 deserves the very opposite character. It aims at the subversion throughout half America and half Europe, of that independence of those institutions which have sprung from the wants, and opinions, and feelings of the mass of their inhabitants; which have been watered by blood, and consecrated by victory; to which those of mature age cling for safety, while the young have been born to them as a birthright.

To this state of things, which has arisen from the movement of the world itself, can one man oppose his will, however inflexible, however preponderating?

Already has the attempt been tried; and in every country to which the Duke of Wellington's policy has extended, his power has been found inadequate to his purposes. In Turkey and in Austria, he has shrunk from fulfilling the expectations he had raised. In France he has been driven to disavow the short-sighted interference he had excited, in creating a ministry whose movements he afterwards found himself unequal to control. In Greece he is forced to co-operate in establishing the independence he had striven to undermine, and which he yet labours to restrict within the narrowest limits. In Portugal he has acted under a mask, which even yet he dares not wholly remove, and, stopping short of the object he had contemplated, is odious to the man whom he persists in serving. Even at home he has been compelled to become the unwilling instrument of the greatest innovation of the age; and to claim credit for a measure to which his political life had been opposed. His strength has been proved, and every where it has bent under the weight imposed upon it : but, were his power commensurate with his will, would it not yet be well to temper its exercise by the recollection that he is mortal? Let pass a few short years, and the very memory of his aspirings shall lie with him in the earth, while the silent and steady progress of human affairs shall continue its uncontrollable march from imperfection to maturity, and from maturity to decay. Take from the British cabinet the one spirit whose impulses it obeys, and say of what elements is the championship of counter-revolution, when once dissolved, to be re-composed? Herein then lies the sin of the system under which England is now governed. It cannot endure. It cannot be harmonized or incorporated with the system of Europe, or of the world, while it exposes us to the hazard and odium of conflict without the possibility of permanent success.

But whatever opinion may be held as to the correctness of these more extended views, it must be admitted by all, that in abandoning the system upon which England had acted in Portugal during three years, the Government of 1828 was called upon to provide for the safety of those Portuguese who had previously been put forwards to prepare the march of its policy.

It has been the curse of our interference to be

always exerted by halves, uniformly stopping short of effecting the purpose it had aimed at, and leaving victims where it had engaged adherents: in this instance, voluntarily leaving them, without an effort in their behalf, when there was neither an obstacle nor a danger in the way of their protection, nor a voice in Europe but would have blessed us for enforcing it. Our system of non-interference has been a cheat from the beginning, exempting every Ministry from doing what they had no mind to, and covering their abandonment of those whom they were inclined to desert. Such was its origin in the affair of Naples—such has been its conclusion in that of Portugal; but in this instance our sense of the consequences is rendered doubly galling by their contrast with those which ensued from the French expedition into Spain. Without examining the principle upon which it was undertaken, it is impossible to overlook the difference of its results. They went to set the King at liberty, to wrest power from the hands of the constitutionalists, to re-establish the despotism in its pristine purity. They did not quit Spain till their objects were secured: they left no victims, and their work has survived their departure.*

* " I believe, Sir, that the French army in Spain is now a " protection to that very party which it was originally called in " to put down. Were the French army suddenly removed at " this precise moment, I verily believe that the immediate " effect of that removal would be to give full scope to the un-

In this country it has been of late too much the practice, to regard its foreign policy less as a national concern, than as the domain of the minister of the day. Each successive Secretary of State has made it his first object to overturn the measures of his predecessor, and thus there has been imprinted upon our counsels a character of vacillation, as fatal to our honour as to our interests. For this misfortune, resulting from the violence of our party spirit, no remedy can be found, unless in the greater fixity of opinions in the Parliament; which not partaking to their full extent the passions of individuals, and having once given its sanction to a course of policy, might be expected to guard the perseverance in that course as essential to the character of the country.

But where Parliament and public opinion are mute, what is left but to despair? One cause of this general apathy may be found in the apprehension of war, which is pushed to such a length, that many who would acquiesce in the whole of the above reasoning, would yet be content to sit down under any load of degradation, rather than encounter the risk of an interruption of the peace. To these persons two answers may be given; one drawn from the particular case—one from general principles.

" bridled rage of a fanatical faction, before which, in the
" whirlwind of intestine strife, the party least in numbers
" would be swept away."—*Speech on the Premiership.*

Upon the particular case it may be stated, that when France invaded Spain in 1823, for the purpose of overthrowing the constitution, she scrupulously abstained from any interference with Portugal, which was at that time governed by a constitution similar to the one she was attacking in Spain. Upon all subsequent occasions, both France, and every other European power, have carefully avoided connecting themselves with Portuguese affairs, in any manner which might give umbrage to this country. For infringing this constant rule of their policy, Mr. Hyde de Neuville was recalled from Lisbon, and for attempting to elude it, Spain found herself reduced to the humiliating necessity of disowning her agents, and of recognising the Portuguese Charter, the object of her fear and hatred.

If upon the arrival of that Charter, when the powers of Europe were free to take their own line, no one was yet found sufficiently hostile or sufficiently hardy to stand forward in opposition to it to the extent of war—what likelihood, what possibility was there, that at a later period when all had recognised it; when Austria (the champion of absolute power) was equally pledged with ourselves to its support; when France had made rapid strides in the ways of constitutional government; when Spain without power in herself, could no longer look to the Ultra party in France for assistance in any enterprise she might engage in, what possibility was

there that our support to the system which all
Europe had then recognised—to the party for whose
safety the faith of Austria had been pledged in
common with our own, could by any combination
of circumstances have engaged us in war? There
were neither grounds upon which it was to arise,
nor a quarter from whence it could spring. Let us
do our Government the justice to acknowledge that
this pretence was not of its contrivance, it origi-
nated with feeble and interested individuals, and
has been adopted by credulity and ignorance. The
particular case being disposed of, let us turn to the
general principle; and upon this it is to be feared
that the acquittal pronounced above cannot be
renewed.

It must be admitted that upon the power of this
country to make war, the present Government has
taken the lowest possible tone—a tone which con-
trasts strangely with that held while Mr. Canning
was a member of the cabinet. Whatever might
have been the real sentiments of that Minister upon
the subject, he had created a belief that England
was prepared to resent either injury or insult, by an
appeal to arms; and what Englishman was there,
who did not feel this conviction in others, as a
security against being called upon to have recourse
to them? When was it ever known that to depre-
cate attack was the way to avoid it? When did
submission to injuries fail to attract a renewal of
them? A state of peace, preserved by a timid and

disgraceful acquiescence, is big with a thousand wars. Unfortunately the consequences of the tone which was held by our Government, are no longer problematical. They spoke too much in earnest to fail in producing conviction, and the fate of Turkey has been the consequence of their frankness.

The time to examine their conduct in that affair has not yet arrived, but whenever the meagre extracts which they cannot withhold, shall have cast a further light upon it, their course therein shall be made as clear as it has now become in the concerns of Portugal; and the war between Russia and the Porte, with all its consequences, shall be traced to its true source, to the vacillations, the irresolution, the timidity, and self-contradictions of the British Government. It shall be proved that it lay with England, either to arrest the war before it had begun, or to limit it in its extent; and that those who thought, by timid compliance, to secure a state of peace, have only arrived at one of sufferance and insecurity, entailing either further sacrifices or ultimate resistance by the sword.

A more fruitful germ of war than could have sprung from the assertion of our rights and of our honour, has been provided in the indisposition which has been created towards us on the continent; and in the opposition wherein we stand to the security of those institutions which the mass of its inhabitants hold dear. Let not the Duke of

Wellington deceive himself; there is no readier source of war than national ill will; and where the belief in the weakness of an enemy is superadded, a pretence for it need not long be wanting.

To be respected, we must assert our rights; to be loved or relied upon, we must protect our adherents; to be secure, we must be confident in our strength, and impress that confidence on others. The elements of these things are not deficient, but they have been barren to us; whether by the misuse made of them by an incapable Ministry, or from a failure in the ancient energy of our national character, is yet a problem.

To arise from our degradation would be but the work of a moment; if we remain in it, the cause must be looked for in ourselves.

FINIS.

Gunnell and Shearman, 13, Salisbury-square.

CPSIA information can be obtained
at www.ICGtesting.com
Printed in the USA
BVHW041703211218
536194BV00005B/27/P